Gondor Writing Centre
Creative Writing Guide
Book 2
Developing Your Story

Plotting

Waking Your Imagination

Keeping Your Reader Hooked

Creative Writing Guide

Book 2

Developing Your Story

Plotting and

Waking Your Imagination

Keeping Your Reader Hooked

© Copyright Elaine Ouston, Australia 2021

Published by

Morris Publishing Australia

http://morrispublishingaustralia.com

ISBN: 978-0-6452388-0-8

All rights reserved. No part of this publication may be reproduced, stored in a retrieval system, or transmitted, in any form or by means, electronic, mechanical, photocopying, recording or otherwise, without the prior written permission of the copyright holder.

CONTENTS:

Chapter One – Plotting a Story   1

Chapter Two – Waking Your Imagination   15

Chapter Three – Keeping Your Readers Hooked   23

Introduction:

Many people tell me they are going to write a book one day and the idea they have will make it a best seller. Now it is great to have that kind of confidence, but when I ask them what knowledge and experience they have as a writer, they say things like, "I was top of my class in English."

If only it was that simple. There is more to writing a best seller than knowing basic English. Having been through the journey from having ideas to turning them into popular books for children, I can tell you it is not that easy.

To me, saying you can write a best-seller without learning about **the craft of story creation** is like saying you are going to do brain surgery without going to medical school.

50% of writing a great work of fiction is imagination and 50% is technical skill on how to build a great story, but these skills can be learned.

Like all professions, to be the best at what you do, you have to work at it. Many people can tell a story, but if it doesn't excite and intrigue the readers on the first page they won't read on.

These skills are needed whatever you are writing – short story, picture book, chapter books for children, poems, memoirs, novels, etc.

This book and the other writing guides will help you learn those skills.

Chapter One

PLOTTING A STORY:

In our first writing guide, *Turning an idea into a story*, we outlined our story. We decided who our main character was, what their goal, motivation, and conflicts were, who would help them on the way, and how the story would end. And we interviewed our characters, so we now know them as well as we know our self, our friends, and our family members. Now, we need to expand on that story line and create a more detailed plot to work with.

Many people believe that writer's block comes from not having a strong plot line, a strong direction to follow. I agree. To me, to write a story of any size without a plan or plot is like going on a journey without a map or GPS. But some writers say they feel restricted by the structure of plot. That doesn't have to be the way it works. A plot is a guideline. It's like planning a journey. If on the way, you see something interesting you can stop and explore that as well.

A story is a series of events recorded in chronological order.

SO, WHAT IS A PLOT?

A plot is a series of events deliberately arranged to reveal the dramatic, thematic, and emotional significance of the events.

We talked last time about the basic formula for stories but before we start on our plot, we'll run through them again.

Protagonist + Objective + Obstacles = Story OR

Character + Desire + Conflict = Story

Someone wants something that is hard to get. Once you understand this, it is much easier to plan your story.

The plot should follow this 5-part sequence:

The Beginning Chapters –Inciting Incident and 3 or 4 scenes that follow.

The Middle Chapters –The Rising Action and The Midpoint Reversal or Point of No Return. (3 or 4 major scenes)

The Climactic Scene (1 or 2 scenes)

The Final Stage - Falling Action (1 or 2 scenes)

The Final Scene – The resolution – The tying up of loose ends.

This is how it looks on a graph.

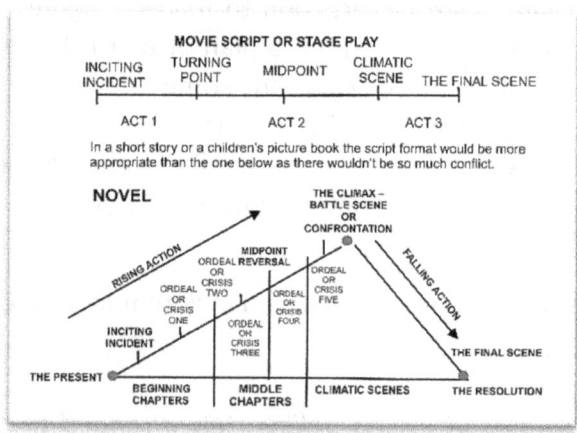

I have included the Three Act script plot formula to show that it is just the same. In a short story or a children's picture book the Three Act script format would be more appropriate than the one below it, as there wouldn't be as much conflict.

There are two ways to write a story:

The Intuitive Approach:

Sometimes called 'writing by the seats of your pants'.

With this approach you set off on a journey with no idea of where you are going, allowing the words to carry you along as they will.

Every time you get stuck, which you will, often, you can use a form of brainstorming to get you going again.

The main problem with this method is that sometimes you can get so stuck you can't get going again, or you end up with a lot of material that must be cut later, thereby wasting time and energy. The questions that you then ask to try to get going, are the same ones you would ask when plotting the story, so why waste time being stuck. Ask them at the start.

The Analytical Approach or Plotting:

Most writers agree that the best way to prepare a story is to plot out the entire story before you write a word, complete with character sketches, chapter-by-chapter and scene-by-scene breakdowns, and conclusions.

Such planning can help with the actual writing process because you know what you are writing about – and it can help you tie up any loose ends.

Then, as you are writing, you develop these plotlines further as new ideas come. You can then adjust your main plotline to suit the story changes before you write the next chapter. This way, you know exactly what you want to happen in the next scene and where the story is going.

However, some people feel it limits them to only writing what was contained in the plot and doesn't leave room for any of those great leaps of the imagination that can take you in all sorts of surprising directions. This doesn't have to happen. As I said earlier, plot lines are only a guide.

A plot is the bare bones of a story — it is a series of events that is driven by the protagonist's attempt to RESOLVE a source of CONFLICT. The protagonist's actions and reactions to a set of problems, obstacles, or ordeals guide the plot.

We are going to look at the questions to ask to lead you through the story for the best possible outcome, and to increase the tension, scene by scene to keep the reader engaged.

But first a quote from someone who knows.

On the subject of plot, Donald Maass, founder of the Donald Maass Literary Agency in New York says: *'If there is one single principle that is central to making any story more powerful, it is simply this:* **Raise the stakes**. *As authors, we get attached to our protagonists. We are tempted to protect them from trouble. That temptation must be resisted.'*

What does that mean? It means, to write a powerful story, be prepared to make life very difficult for your characters.

Remember, without conflict there is no story.

Another quote I like comes from P.G. Wodehouse I think he said it best: 'The principle I always go on in writing a novel is to think of the characters in terms of actors in a play. I say to myself, if a big name were playing this part, and if he found that after a strong first act, he had practically nothing to do in the second act, he would walk out.

'I believe the only way a writer can keep himself up to the mark is by examining each story quite coldly before he starts writing it and asking himself if it is an interesting and engaging story.

'I mean, once you go saying to yourself, "This is a pretty weak plot as it stands, but I'm such a hell of a writer that my magic touch will make it okay," you're sunk. If they aren't in interesting situations, characters can't be major characters, not even if you have the rest of the troop talk their heads off about them.' (Interview, *The Paris Review*, Issue 64, Winter 1975)" (best known for his books on Jeeves and Bertie Wooster)

P.G. Wodehouse

A plot works in two ways – *what* is happening (the sequence of events) and *why* it is happening (cause and effect).

Character and plot are entwined, because the personality of your characters will determine how they react to any given situation.

That is why it is so important to do your character interview and know your characters well.

THE IMPORTANT QUESTIONS TO ASK ARE:

For the inciting incident and the chapters up to the climactic scene:

What are the worst possible thing that could happen to our character to change his life?

What are the worst things that could happen while he tried to fix it?

What are the best possible outcomes from those events?

Write a list of at least six of the worst possible things that could happen to your main character, starting with the inciting incident.

Try to write them in order of intensity and importance, remembering we are trying to make the tension and action rise as we go.

Just write them simply like: He could fall off a cliff. He could get hooked on drugs. His girlfriend could turn him down, etc.

Then under each, write how your character could overcome these conflicts.

The question you will ask for the climactic scene is:

How will he overcome the major conflict?

What is the outcome of this event?

Write down how he would overcome this final conflict and what the outcome would be for him and his adversary (if there is one).

And for the resolution:

What is the best outcome for our hero?

Write down how your hero's life was changed by this experience.

We will then go on and expand these events into scenes.

These are the questions you will answer in each scene, starting with the inciting incident:

Where is my character (Physically and emotionally)?

Where would he logically go from there?

How can I up the stakes? (What is the worst thing that could happen to him now?)

What am I trying to express or communicate with this scene?

What is the best possible outcome from this event?

How was my character changed by this experience?

To help you make sense of that, let's look at an example.

Following is an outline and an extract from my plot for my YA novel, *Restoring Destiny,* and then the scene that plays out from the last plot point read.

Outline: The story takes place in the land of Navaah. The race of people is average size. An evil man from the land of giants has invaded and overthrown the King. He now rules the land. He imprisoned the King and his loyal followers.

Twins, a boy and girl, fifteen, grow up with an old couple in a country area in East Nevaah. They are home schooled and not allowed to mix with other people. Their names are Rais (boy) and Kanda (girl). They wear an amulet of pure gold with an engraving of an owl. When questioned about it, their guardians told them to keep it hidden but wear it at all times.

Unknown to them, the twins are the children of Baldasarre, The Oracle of the former King of Navaah and a magic healer, Edalene.

The twins were spirited away during the overthrow and put in the care of an old couple in East Nevaah. The children are unaware of their origins, and the fact that they have been the subject of a search by the evil ruler for twelve years.

The plot points for the inciting incident: Just before their 16th birthday a scout from the palace who is loyal to the imprisoned King, comes to the farm. He tells their guardian, Nona, that their mother is to be executed at the next full moon and the twins with their magic skills are the only ones who can save her.

Nona sends him out to find the old servant of the children's father, Briador, who placed the twins in their care.

The twins listen in but miss the first part about the execution. They hear Nona instruct the scout to find Briador who she believes is living in a town not far away. They are puzzled by the whole thing as they have forgotten who he is. Nona refuses to tell them what the visit was about and who the messenger was.

The scout is caught by Yaholo's henchmen and tortured for the children's whereabouts.

Major scene two plot: Two strange men in the uniform of the evil ruler's troops arrive at the door enquiring about the children. Their male guardian, Pap, who opened the door to them, denies their presence. Beside Pap is the children's pet liogon (an invented animal that is half lion and half dog). His menacing presence is all that stops the troops from barging into the house.

The soldier declares that the scout is dead, but before he died, he told them of the children's whereabouts. Pap is told that he and his wife will be killed if he doesn't allow them to search the house. Nona and the children are listening, and Nona instructs the twins to run to the nearest town and find their father's servant. They don't really want to leave the old folk to face the stranger alone but know that they are all in danger if they stay.

They scurry away from the house through a tunnel they have built in a dense thicket of bushes at the rear of the house. The tunnel leads to the bank of the river not far away.

Let's break down that scene plot to see how it answers our questions.

Where are our characters and what are they doing?

Physically: *The twins are hiding in the house with Nona while Pap answers the door to the stranger.*

Emotionally: *They are scared of what is happening.*

Where would the characters logically go from there? *They would hide and be discovered or try to save their guardians and be captured.*

How can I up the stakes: *Send them on a dangerous journey into a world they have never seen with the evil ruler's troops chasing them.*

What is the best possible outcome from this event? *They escape this situation.*

What am I trying to express or communicate with this scene? *I am trying to create a sense of urgency, a hook to make the reader want to read on and find out what happens next.*

How were my characters changed by this experience? *They are now out on their own after being cloistered all their life, and fearful, and uncertain of what to do next.*

From that outline and the character interviews for each character involved, I sat and started writing. Let's look at how that paragraph plays out as a full scene.

This is the scene that was written from that plot outline.

'By the time night threw its cloak of darkness over the light of day, they were in the kitchen with Nona, helping clean up after the meal. Nobosi suddenly rose from his position by the fire and bounded to the front door, a growl low in his throat warned them of an approaching stranger. The front door creaked as a huge fist pounded it. Pictures rattled on the wall.

Nobosi scratched at the door, barking and growling menacingly. Pap rose stiffly and went to see who disturbed their peace.

The twins wanted to follow, but Nona held them back. All three hid in the living room to listen.

"The twins, I know they are here. Bring them to me," a strange voice thundered.

"I ... don't know who you mean," Pap said glancing over his shoulder and putting his hand on Nobosi's head for reassurance. The low throaty growl coming from Nobosi was all that stopped the man from pushing past him.

"Don't play games with me. Your scout is dead, but before he died, he told us what we wanted to know. If you don't call off that liogon and let us in to search the house, you and your wife will die."

"If the children were found here, we would all die anyway," Pap shouted.

Nona pulled them back from the hall doorway. She knew he had said that for her benefit. Through the window, in the faint light of the rising moon, they could see another man dressed in a dark blue uniform striding towards the back of the house.

Her face pale and tears streaming down her cheeks, Nona whispered, "Go! Go now, out the side window. I was afraid this might happen. I have packed some of your things. Go to Adaya and find Briador."

Rais hesitated. "But Nona ... what will happen to you if we go?"

"If you go, we will be fine. If you are found here, we will all die," Nona declared.

No more needed to be said. With a quick hug, the twins raced for the side window, grabbing their leather packs as they ran.

Outside, they sped for a concealed tunnel they had created through the dense thicket of bushes that led to the river.

They had used it many times as a means of escape from the watchful eyes of their guardians. Now, to hide their escape route they replaced the bush that hid the entrance and scampered as quietly as possible for the river.

You can see that my plot outline was just the bare bones of that scene. The dialogue and action of all the characters was worked out and written from that basic outline, and the character profile. So even with the plot outline, there is a lot of work to do and a lot of room for creativity.

Now it's your turn. Answer the questions below for each of the scenes from the story outline you wrote following the 9 building blocks in the last guide. Expand on each with more scenes as listed below and create the plot for each scene.

If you are writing them on paper, put them on separate pieces of paper or on separate pages. This allows you to arrange them later in order of importance and intensity if you need to. Remember you are raising the tension and action with every scene to keep the reader hooked.

Here again are the questions you will need to ask for each scene and the guideline to how many major scenes you will need for a novel, with more detail.

QUESTIONS: *Where is my character (Physically and emotionally)?*

Where would he logically go from here?

How can I up the stakes? (What is the worst thing that could happen to him now?)

What am I trying to express or communicate with this scene?

What is the best possible outcome from this event?

How was my character changed by this experience?

THE SCENES:

The Beginning Chapters – Inciting Incident and 3 or 4 scenes that follow.

The opening scene: Remember to start your story with a dramatic opening that provides the hook that makes the reader want to read more. You can show the normal life of the main characters later.

The hook can be just a few words that foreshadows a coming Inciting Incident as in Mathew Reilly's – *Six Sacred Stones*: the novel begins:

'On the day his farm was attacked with overwhelming force, Jack West Jr had slept till around 7.00am.'

The next couple of pages then tells us of the normal life of this character – his family – where he lives and why – what his background is etc.

But we keep reading because we know there is going to be an attack and we want to know when, why and how. But don't drag this section out too long or you will lose your reader. Get to the action scene after a couple of pages.

The remainder of this first chapter of any book should tell what the incident was and how our character reacted to it. How it changed our protagonist's life and what the character plans to do about it – their Goal and Motivation.

This should be followed up by 2 or 3 scenes that give the reader an insight into how the main character responds to the inciting incident and what action they will take to rectify the situation.

Take time now to work out the plot for these scenes using the questions above.

The Middle Chapters – The Rising Action and The Midpoint Reversal (3 or 4 major scenes)

Here we show a series of conflicts and obstacles our character has to overcome, ordeals to undergo, lessons to be learnt, and revelations to be understood. This section gives details of the journey, with each scene being more dramatic than the last.

This leads us to the **Point of No Return** we talked about in the 9 building blocks – a crucial or decisive moment in the story that has a powerful effect on the protagonist. This is the scene where your protagonist feels overwhelmed and must decide if they have the strength and determination to go on. Is the goal worth the effort? This crisis stops the middle chapter from sagging. This can be a physical obstruction or an emotional one.

Take time now to work out the plot for these scenes using the questions above.

The Climactic Scene – (1 or 2 scenes)

This is where we give details of the lead up to the final confrontation – the BIG MOMENT when tension reaches its height – the point in which the hero must not only face, and defeat, his enemy, but also his greatest fear.

Take time now to work out the plot for these scenes using the questions we talked about earlier.

The Final Stage – Falling Action (1 or 2 scenes)

Here questions are answered, and problems solved. This is where we learn more about the motivation of the antagonists and reveal any twists not already shown. It is usually much shorter than the previous series of events.

Take time now to work out the plot for these scenes using the questions above.

The Final Scene – The resolution – The tying up of loose ends. Here we reveal how the experience has changed your hero, and what 'normal' will be for him now. It should show some growth or change in your character.

We are all changed by every major experience in life. To make it believable, your character should too.

It's where the hero rides happily off into the sunset if it is a single book. If it is a series, this is where you put the hook to make readers want to buy the next book.

Take time now to work out the plot for this scene using the questions above.

You can see that understanding the basic narrative arc of a story can make sure your story does not sag in the middle, fizzle out at the end, or drone on for too long at the beginning. Editors tell me the 'too long beginning' is the most common mistakes in manuscripts. They say that in most manuscripts, the first two or three chapters are back-story and can be left out. And the information woven into the story if it is needed. Formulating a strong plot, can help prevent a dull beginning, and hook your reader from the first paragraph.

More scenes will be created between these major scenes as you write but it is vital to plot the main action and emotion before you start.

Let's now look at how to enlarge on the plot, use our imagination to make it exciting and memorable, and at ways to keep the reader hooked from beginning to end.

Chapter Two

Waking Your Imagination

We are all born with an imagination. You only have to watch small children at play to see that. They can imagine themselves to be anything that they want. I'm sure you have heard them. They pretend that they are their favourite heroes and give the other kids roles. They then go on to create a scene and act it out.

Sadly, some of us had our imaginations reined in during our upbringing. But your imagination can be stimulated. So what happened to that imagination? In my opinion and experience, some parents, some teachers, and others stifled it. When I was a child I had a wonderful loving mother, but she was a practical down-to-earth person. I was the kind of child who had a strong imagination and if I said something she considered not possible or practical, she would tell me to 'stop talking nonsense'.
Fortunately for me, my father was just as imaginative as I was.

Other people who didn't have their imagination squashed create all the amazing inventions we take for granted. Imagine where the world would be without these people who can look at a problem and come up with a solution. To do this they have to use their imagination and believe that everything is possible. It is the same in writing.

I was lucky. My dad nurtured my imagination and at the second school I went to the teacher did too.

When I started to write stories for children, I had no trouble coming up with an exciting plot. In fact, I had to rein it in a bit as

I realised I had to make it believable, even if it was fantasy.

One of my first editors told me I had a great imagination and asked me where I got my ideas. I told her I got my ideas from my wild imagination that my father had allowed me to keep. I told her a little of my childhood. She nodded and said she wasn't so lucky. I felt sorry for her. How sad it would be to have all the knowledge she has of the technical aspects of how to write a great story, but not the imagination to dream one up.

So today, we are going to help you stimulate the imagination you were born with. Let's look at other writers who have allowed their imagination to create great stories and explore how they did that.

The best-selling novels in the world all have one thing in common. The storyline is larger than life. In a major fantasy, spy, thriller, or crime novel, the stakes are huge. Often it is not only the life of the main character that is at stake, but that of his family, community, or even nation. The characters are also larger than life.

This is true even in children and young adult fiction.

In many major women's novels, the stake may be emotional – personal fulfilment, losing or finding the ideal partner, drama with a child, etc. But it must not be the boring stuff of everyday life, the heroines' lust, longings and passions must be imbued by their creators with such fierce and unrelenting intensity that what is at issue for them is as powerfully depicted as a murder or mayhem in a crime novel. There can be no shrinking violets in this kind of story.

Anyone can come up with an idea for a story, but to turn that idea into a best seller, you must use your imagination to come up with a way to make it LARGER THAN LIFE.

As I have said before, the simple structure of a story is a character who wants to achieve something and someone or something trying to stop him.

Remember, that doesn't have to be an enemy, it can be an emotion, the weather, or any other obstacle you can throw in their way.

Albert Zuckerman, in his book, *Writing the Block Buster Novel,* says, 'Combine "high concept" with a strong dramatic question and you may have a better chance of coming up with a BIG BOOK.' (High concept being a radical or even somewhat outlandish premise or plot.) He says, 'For a novel to be big, the reader must empathize with (or better, care passionately about) one or even two or three of the main characters.'

Let's look at a book with a high concept. In *The First Wives Club* by Olivia Goldsmith, three middle-aged women are tossed aside by their callous multi-millionaire husbands, who take up with younger women. The badly treated ex-wives are provoked into seeking revenge. If you haven't seen this film, you should. It is a perfect example of taking an idea – revenge – and taking it to the extreme. Here is a review that explains the storyline.

'There ought to be some kind of retribution, some way to even the score. Let's make sure they pay a price.' These are the words of a veritable Park Avenue Princess in Goldsmith's sharp, vitriolic, funny, and exceedingly commercial debut novel – all about what happens when three abandoned society wives get mad. The wives are a little slow to cut loose because, as one of them points out, 'We are a generation of masochists.' Besides, their divorces have laid them low.

'Good girl, Annie Paradise, still thinks she loves her soon-to-be ex, advertising-whiz, Aaron, who gambled away their Down's syndrome daughter's trust fund in a bum stock deal.

He then shacks up with – of all people – <u>Annie's old sex-therapist.</u>

'Meanwhile, her Greenwich Village pal, Elise Atchison, a faded but still beautiful movie star and fantastically wealthy heiress, puts up with the promiscuity of her "empty suit," Bill, for years until – to add insult to injury – he decides to walk with an <u>anorexically thin, cocaine-snorting performance artist.</u>

'And Brenda, the wise-cracking former wife of crass, appliance-peddling millionaire Morty the Madman, takes solace in cookies and pies when she is tossed aside for <u>a slender, gentile social climber.</u>

'After one of their group suicides and the girls get together for lunch, they determine to see to it that there's justice for first wives. Their goals? Morty broke, Bill castrated, and Aaron abandoned – most of which they accomplish with the help of Elise's dough, the Securities and Exchange Commission, and a US senator.

'Along the way, they find themselves new beaux, laughs, tears, and vastly improved lives. They never had it so good, nor do most real, down-to-earth first wives. But this is fantasy, with warm, cuddly female characters and larger-than-life, utterly villainous men.

Moreover, the novel mainlines into a vein of pure bile – which can't help but produce heady effects on those millions of women who know exactly what Goldsmith's talking about.'

You will have noticed that, following the 'larger than life' premise, the three wives, and the women the husbands left them for were *not ordinary people*, and they were all totally different personalities. The wives consisted of an exceptionally rich ex-movie star, a good girl type with a Downs syndrome child, and a wise-cracking down-to-earth woman. The 'other women' were <u>Annie's old sex-therapist,</u> <u>anorexically thin, cocaine-snorting performance artist</u> and <u>a slender, gentile social climber.</u>

The 'High concept' in this film is not the revenge, but the way it is achieved. The method used is so devious and over-the-top that it almost seems like it would be possible.

Albert says that a BIG BOOK needs to be built on highly dramatic situations and plots that include bizarre and surprising actions that lead from one confrontation to another – with the confrontations escalating each time. The setting is just as important. He adds that readers of popular books enjoy escaping into the minds, hearts and the ups-and-downs of fictional characters, but they also like to be drawn into new, unfamiliar, and exotic locations.

Let's look at another example: In her novel, *The Girl in the Basement*, Dianne Bates has taken the premise that a girl is kidnapped by a psychopath and locked in a basement. This book takes a simple idea of a kidnapping and turns it into a page-turning, spine-chilling thriller.

The book was inspired by a photo and news article. It showed two young people, a teenage girl, and a boy about 10, tied up in the back of a van. The photo was found in a car park in America.

The girl was eventually identified but never found and the identity of the boy remains a mystery. Dianne sat looking at the photo in the newspaper, wondering who would do that and why. Why would he take two young people? If he had kidnapped the girl only, you could assume that the motivation was sex, but there was also a 10 year-old-boy.

What she came up with was amazing.

The story took a lot of research. To tell the story as grippingly as she did, she had to work out what kind of person would commit the crime and what his motivation could be.

To develop the characters for this novel would have taken the same kind of research I did to come up with the personalities of criminals for our character workshop and guide.

Once a personality was chosen, research into how that kind of personality would behave would be necessary, and what his background was like to make him into the person he is. We are all who we are because of our background and up-bringing. She also researched stories of other girls who had been kidnapped in many places in the world.

How do you write a story like this LARGER-THAN-LIFE story? One of the ways is to take an idea and ask yourself, 'What if?

Di's *'What If'* moments would be: *What if* he didn't want to kidnap them for sex? If not that, then what? That led her to the thought, *What if* he wanted to recreate a family he had lost?

The next question was *What if* she tried to escape. And of course, she did. Di used a plot graph such as the one we covered in the plotting and building blocks guide to make sure that each time she tried, the stakes and the violence escalated. After the last attempt, during which she was almost killed, Di had to stop and say, *What if* she decides to be more cunning and play along with his wishes to stay safe and gain his trust? But when this led to no chance to escape, the final question had to be *what if* she decided that the only way to get away would be to kill him?

How would she do that, and would she survive the attempt?

Many more *'What if'* moments would have been used to build the story. Many answers would have been abandoned as too boring, or too normal to make the book as exciting as it is.

Here is one of the many great reviews that this book received:

Dianne Bates' new thriller The Girl in the Basement is a page turner that once started you will not be able to put down. Sixteen-year-old Libby is snatched off the streets by a man and spends the next few months swinging between terror and calculating her escape. Extra dimensions are added when Psycho Man, as Libby thinks of him, kidnaps a young boy to complete his family.

Bates pulls off a major writing coup: she successfully flits between the heads of Libby and her kidnapper giving us insights into the motivations and emotions of both. A lesser writer would have failed in this, but it is testament to Bates' skill that the head hopping enhances the story. Memories of her loving family strikingly contrast with Psycho Man's warped version.

The mind of a psychopath is an unnerving thing to delve into. The accommodation of his distorted sense of reality into his life view is chilling, and fatal to others. If you are after a light read, then this is not the book for you. There is violence, brutal at times, and more than one death. The violence is always in context and never gratuitous.

This is a book for older teen readers or adults. While the events in this book are fictional, it is a disturbing reminder of the depths humans can plunge to. Fortunately, it is also a reminder of the strength of character and tenacity we can summon in the face of the cruellest circumstances. The characters in this book are definitely LARGER THAN LIFE.

You should read this book as an example of how to create stand-out characters.

The children and young adult novels that come to mind that contain a High Concept and Larger-Than-Life characters are *Harry Potter,* and *The Hunger Games* but there are many more. It works in all genres.

So, we have established that the most important thing you need to create a story that is larger than life is a good imagination.

And that the way to stimulate that imagination is to ask *What if?*

Now it's your turn to try doing that. I want you to go back to your plot outline and look again at what you imagined the major scenes would include and ask yourself *'what if?'* to see if you can 'up the stakes' and make your story LARGE THAN LIFE. Ideally, it should end with a twist. Now we move on to the final stage before you write your story; how to keep your reader hooked.

Chapter Three

Keeping Your Reader hooked

Whatever you write – fiction, nonfiction, or blog posts, you have a singular goal: to make the reader want to keep on reading. No matter what you are writing, there are all kinds of techniques to keep your reader hooked from one chapter to the next. We will examine the best way to do this.

Think about what makes you stay glued to the pages of a novel until your eyes can't stay open anymore.

These are the things that keep me reading:

Interesting characters that I care about.

A well developed and intriguing plot/story line.

Rising tension created by questions I want answered. This draws me further into the story.

The writer unravelling tantalising clues in each chapter to keep me hooked.

Breaks in scenes and at the ends of chapters that leave me wanting to know more.

Foreshadowing of up-coming events of which the main character is unaware.

Let's break that down and examine each one.

INTERESTING CHARACTERS YOU CARE ABOUT:

I can't emphasise enough the importance of a well-developed and rounded character. Many people tell me they stop reading a story because they couldn't care less about what happens to the main character. If they don't care what happens to them, you can't build suspense. Make sure you know your character well before you start and give him or her the characteristics that will make your reader care what happens.

During the first few paragraphs, you must introduce the character and the situation they are in, but more importantly, you must tell the reader how the character feels about that situation. And continue to do so all through the story. Draw the reader in so they feel like they're part of the story. In a way, they become that character on the page. Have you ever felt that way?

USING EMOTION:

How do we make the reader care? Use emotion. Tell the reader how and why the characters have trouble with the obstacles.

If the reader doesn't know how they feel about the event, and how much they fear what could happen next, they won't relate to your characters, and you will lose their interest.

You build suspense best by mixing emotion with action. Here is an example of building suspense and tension in a scene using emotion, taken from Cynthia Vespia's novel, *Demon Hunter – The Chosen One*:

(description and action) *His heavy boots made a sick-wet sound as they slapped the soft earth. Debris and chunks of dirt blew into our faces, taunting us with the desire to cough aloud but we remained as still as statues. Our eyes kept trained on the man's every move.*

The knife was outstretched in his hands. Almost all of the blood had dried, giving its color a dark crimson masking, rather than the brighter sheen of a fresh kill. The remaining liquid congealed at the tip pulling one solitary, fat droplet down off the knife. It plummeted fast and found its landing on the back of my hand.

(emotion and description) Warmth and cold both blanketed me in the same sensation as the blood sat soaking upon my skin. Both Tuck and I sat staring at the droplet in stark terror, daring not to move one single inch. That one small drop of blood marked what true danger we were exposed to.

(action) Finally, I managed to pull my gaze away and regard the stranger before us. (emotion) My blood ran cold as the man's eyes rained down upon me, locked against my own. (description) They were dark orbs, almost as dark as night, and they held within them just a touch of madness staring out from under his full brimmed hat.

Notice how the emotions intertwine with description to move the story forward. This inner dialogue is so important. Don't just tell us what is happening; if you tell us how the character feels about what is happening, we are more involved in the story. This is the only way we will truly get to know your protagonist. This can be done in many ways. One way is through the thoughts or speech of the character, but it can also be through narrative.

To summarise: Make your protagonists strong and make them act with courage against the challenges you throw at them. Make the reader care about your main characters by letting them know the characters inner thoughts and feelings. You could also introduce a second main character for another point of view, enabling structural breaks from each point of view at tense moments.

As I said before, your scenes should also end in a way that builds towards an event, or poses a question, or an expectation of what's to follow, creating rising action.

Question created in the example above: What will happen next?

CREATING RISING TENSION:

Tension is primarily developed by posing questions that the reader wants answered. The first page of a novel will contain the inciting incident and present a character in some kind of trouble or dilemma; the immediate questions then are who is this person, what kind of trouble is he/she in, and why? It is then the job of the first chapter to give the background and increase the tension by telling the reader what the character has to lose by facing the problem that has been thrust on him.

Longer-term questions include how the character will extricate himself, and what the fallout might be. Questions are best presented on both a scene-by-scene and overall story-arc level, with minor questions posed and answered most frequently. This satisfies the reader's desire for information and understanding, while continuing to build the tension slowly towards the story's climax.

Structure also helps build suspense. There must be suspense in each scene to keep the reader engaged. If you are writing from the point of view of two characters, rather than allowing a scene to come to a natural conclusion, a writer can break it early, leaving a character in danger or about to learn important information, and go to the second point of view. When the reader is made to spend time in another character's point of view, the delayed return to the first character builds anticipation and suspense.

Here is a scene from Butterfly by Sonya Hartnett. Plum has just been told that her next-door neighbour and her brother are running away together. Her reaction in speech and thought tells us a how she is feeling, but Sonya's narrative tells us a great deal more. This passage contains the best use of simile and metaphor I have ever read.

It also creates foreshadowing, which creates rising tension. Watch for the way she uses many senses as she describes what Plum is feeling.

Plum's mouth opens and shuts. Everything is helter-skelter. Her eyes feel pulled unnaturally wide; her ears hear a hollow ring. Her whole body hurts like it's been thrown into a wall. This is the worst thing that's happened to her. 'I don't want Justin to go away,' she says, in a voice like a gravel road. 'I don't want you to go away, either. What about me?'

"*Oh Aria, you'll be fine. I know you – I know how strong you are. You think you're not, but you are. And you can visit during the school holidays – wouldn't you like that?'*

'"*No, I'd like it better if you stayed here.'*

'*I know.' Maureen winces. 'But it is all planned now. Maybe when you're old enough, you could spend a few months with us or even a year? I would love that – wouldn't you?'*

The prospect sparks no enthusiasm in Plum. She sits like a toy that's been too tightly wound, packed with energy yet paralysed, her gaze flat and unseeing. 'I didn't know about any of this.'

'*No, but you almost did. Do you remember thinking that Justin had a secret? Well, I'm his secret. Everything I just told you is our secret. No one knows about any of this yet – you're the first. Isn't that exciting?'*

Plum is being hit by waves of shock that are knocking her down and tumbling her over, making it difficult to think; in the distance is rising the greatest wave, which will arrive in wrath and thunder. This tidal wave is sucking oxygen from the room, leaving her for a moment, muted and suppressed.

In Butterfly, even though the scene has ended, from the line, *'Plum is being hit by waves of shock...'* there is the expectation of more to come. The suspense in Butterfly is created by the readers expectation that Plum will react badly, and is increased by the words, "... in the distance is rising the greatest wave, which will arrive in wrath and thunder". At that point we believe Plum is about to explode and vent her anger and frustration. But it doesn't come then. Hartnett cleverly breaks to a section of the POV of Justin with it still hanging, and then comes back to the story with Plum.

So, try introducing a second main character for another point of view, enabling structural breaks from each point of view at tense moments.

PLANTING SEEDS:

Readers put together fragments of information in an effort to imagine what might happen. The writer can make this harder by withholding details or presenting them out of order, causing more uncertainty. Ambiguity helps hide the true meaning of a clue. The writer puts information forward in such a way that the reader may miss it or may not realise its significance.

For instance, if you were planning a murder as a climax, you might mention in a description of the room, the gun that hangs on the wall in the study or the handgun in the bedside table that makes one of the characters nervous. You might also describe how a frustrated victim feels when clutching a carving knife.

This way you have planted several seeds so that when the victim has had enough, the reader will wonder if they will be tempted to use one of the weapons mentioned, and which one will be used.

Then of course, for a twist, you would use a totally different way to kill the antagonist. A push down the stairs, an accident, a heart attack etc. or have someone else do the deed.

Sometimes the narrative hints at a future occurrence or plants a red herring to throw the reader off the true villain.

Readers may recognise such information as 'planted' for later use, but also remember that writers can introduce false plants, known as 'snares', which turn out to have no later relevance.

How many times in a murder mystery do the writers plant a suspect by having a character say, 'I'm glad he is dead', the reader then has to consider whether that character might actually have done it. This thinking leads to a range of questions in their mind and in the mind of the detectives about why, and if so how. The reality could be that it's merely an idle quote, unrelated to the actual murder, just an expression of the opinion of the speaker of the dead character.

Snares: This act of questioning and waiting to discover the answer increases suspense. If you plant several of these 'snares', as all good mystery writers do, you keep the reader guessing. Don't eliminate all suspects until the big reveal. This holds the suspense.

BUILDING EXPECTATION:

When readers imagine what might happen in a story, they consider possible outcomes and assess their likelihood. The fewer apparent solutions to a character's dilemmas, and the more serious the threat, the higher the suspense will be. Furthermore, when readers are unable to work out any solution, they tend to feel an even more intense level of suspense.

However, total certainty that a bad outcome will befall a liked character produces disappointment and sadness rather than suspense. It's important therefore to keep some hope alive in the reader.

Ensure that you unravel little clues as you go to keep the reader looking forward, otherwise the text will seem long and the end too far away. By the beginning of the climactic scene, a reader should feel like they know the ending, but you would, of course, throw a twist in here to prove them wrong.

The ending of a novel plays a crucial role in satisfying a reader. Readers form ideas, no matter how vague, about what fates particular characters deserve, and an ending that fails to deliver this disappoints. If you have invested a lot of work in making the reader love your characters, killing them off would not be a satisfying end for the reader.

After the resolution, the readers may mentally look back over the text to see how it worked, and because they have been constructing their own idea of the ending through the narrative, SOME OF the clues, in hindsight, must add up.

Summary: Don't explain too much, instead fill the text with plants and snares, and leave questions unanswered in as many scenes as possible. But plant the clues often and as subtly as possible so that the revelations of the ending will make sense and so the reader is satisfied with the result.

PACE:

Pace is important in keeping readers hooked. Learning how to write a narrative with the right pace is one of the most crucial writing skills there is. Get it wrong and you are seriously jeopardizing your chances of success. How do we create a good pace?

Action scenes should have active voice, short words, strong verbs and nouns, and short sharp sentences to add pace.

Description of setting and people, flash backs, or spoken memories slow pace.

If you really want to grasp how to write a narrative with the correct pace, think about reading a novel as taking a trip downstream in a boat. You need plenty of white water for excitement. And you need calmer stretches in between for the readers to draw breath and take in the beautiful scenery.

Usually, you would write the first part of an action scene up to the climax in the fast pace and then the resolution in a slow pace. But don't forget to add some calm water scenes between the action scenes to give the reader a break.

A novel that is *all* fast rapids or *all* calm water is not interesting. Control the pace, control the story, and you control the reader.

Foreshadowing is the act of giving a hint of what is to come. As I mentioned before, it is best used at the end of a scene or chapter. Because it is normally hinting at something that is to come that the main character doesn't know about, it gives the reader a sense of power.

Remember the line in Butterfly, '... in the distance is rising the greatest wave, which will arrive in wrath and thunder', that is foreshadowing written by a master.

I use foreshadowing at the end of some scenes and all chapters and at the end of my series to create a desire to read on and to buy the next book.

The best way to be sure you understand what we have talked about today is to start writing the first scene in your story.

Play out the scene in your mind as you write, moment to moment, just as if it is happening now. When you have finished, read it over, and adjust until you feel your heart quicken with dread or anticipation.

When you finish the first draft, check to make sure it contains all of the points mentioned in this guide. Use *what if?* to up the stakes if you think it needs it.

But my most important tip for you is this: have fun!

Writing, like life, should be an enjoyable journey. Don't get bogged down with trying to make the first draft perfect. The tips I've presented here are a starting point to help you on that journey.

Write your story and make sure you enjoy it. The hard work of perfecting it comes in the edit and rewrite.

Our next guide is on developing strong and memorable character. In it you will learn the many personality types there are and how to use them to make your characters interesting and memorable.

If you are interested in mystery or crime writing, the guide will also contain criminal profiles and what drives them to commit crimes.

Even if you're not writing crime, I think we can all learn something valuable by looking at how a profiler works out the personality types of people who committed crimes from their actions. This will help us develop our characters.

Reading the character guide will help you improve on the profiles you have created for your major characters.

www.ingramcontent.com/pod-product-compliance
Lightning Source LLC
Chambersburg PA
CBHW062004180426
43198CB00036B/2368